02/17

D1237568

I Love Sports

Bowling

by Cari Meister

Bullfrog Books

Ideas for Parents and Teachers

Bullfrog Books let children practice reading informational text at the earliest reading levels. Repetition, familiar words, and photo labels support early readers.

Before Reading

- Discuss the cover photo. What does it tell them?

- Look at the picture glossary together. Read and discuss the words.

Read the Book

- "Walk" through the book and look at the photos. Let the child ask questions. Point out the photo labels.

- Read the book to the child, or have him or her read independently.

After Reading

- Prompt the child to think more. Ask: Have you ever gone bowling? Did you get better the more you bowled?

Bullfrog Books are published by Jump!
5357 Penn Avenue South
Minneapolis, MN 55419
www.jumplibrary.com

Library of Congress Cataloging-in-Publication Data

Names: Meister, Cari.
Title: Bowling / by Cari Meister.
Description: Minneapolis, Minnesota: Jump!, Inc. [2017] | Series: Bullfrog Books. I Love Sports Includes index. | Audience: Ages: 5-8.
Audience: Grades: K to Grade 3.
Identifiers: LCCN 2016008094 (print)
LCCN 2016009459 (ebook)
ISBN 9781620313589 (hardcover: alk. paper)
ISBN 9781624964053 (ebook)
Subjects: LCSH: Bowling—Juvenile literature.
Classification: LCC GV903.5.M45 2016 (print)
LCC GV903.5 (ebook) | DDC 794.6—dc23
LC record available at http://lccn.loc.gov/2016008094

Editor: Jenny Fretland VanVoorst
Series Designer: Ellen Huber
Book Designer: Leah Sanders
Photo Researchers: Kirsten Chang, Leah Sanders

Photo Credits: Adobe Stock, cover, 23tr; Age Fotostock, 5, 19, 20–21; Fotolia, 6–7, 23bl; Getty, 14–15, 18, 23tl; iStock, 23mr; Shutterstock, cover, 1, 3, 12, 13, 16–17, 22, 23br, 24; Superstock, 8–9, 23ml; Thinkstock, 4, 10–11.

Printed in the United States of America at Corporate Graphics in North Mankato, Minnesota.

Table of Contents

Let's Bowl!

Pick a ball.

Grab some shoes.

Let's bowl!

5

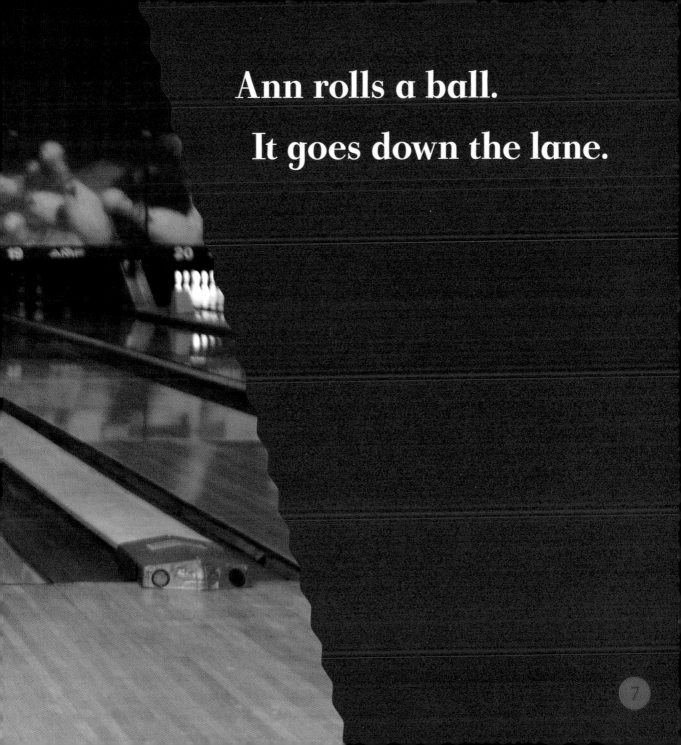

Ann rolls a ball.

It goes down the lane.

Oh, no!
It goes in the gutter.

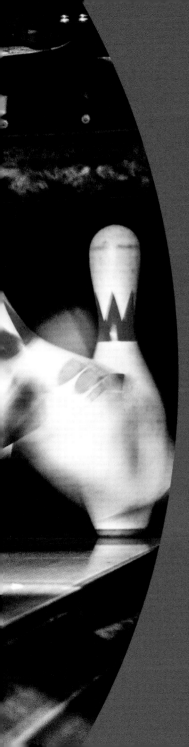

Ann rolls her second ball.

Crash!

The ball knocks
down seven pins.

Ann gets seven points.

ball
return

The ball goes in the pit.
It comes back on the return.

The pins get restacked.

bumper

Now Joe is up.

He rolls with bumpers.

His ball cannot go in the gutter.

Three pins fall.

Now he rolls
his second ball.

Joe hits the
rest of the pins.

He gets a spare!

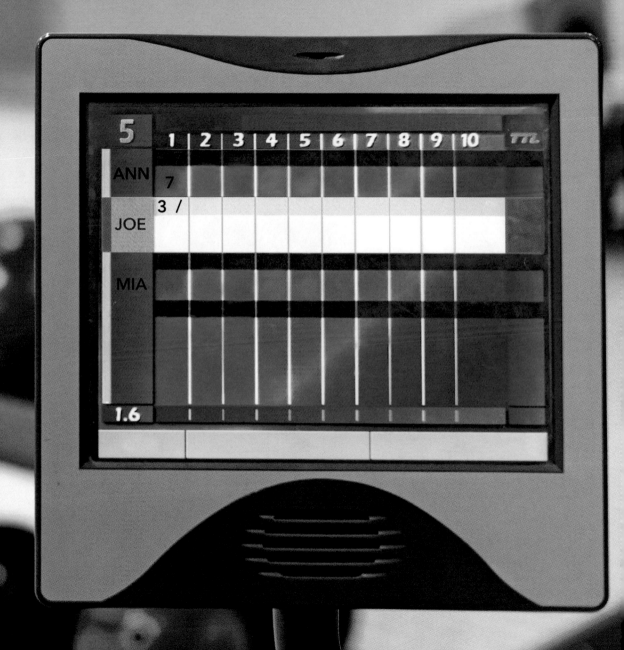

It is Mia's turn.
She rolls the ball.

18

She hits all the pins.

It's a strike!

Do you want to try?

Grab a ball.

Bowling is fun!

At the Bowling Alley

scoreboard

pins

lane

gutter

ball return

Picture Glossary

bumpers
Long bars or pieces of foam that are placed in bowling gutters.

pins
Slender, pear-shaped objects that serve as targets in bowling.

gutter
A channel that runs beside the bowling lane that can trap the ball.

spare
When a player knocks down all of the pins on their second ball.

lane
A track down which bowlers roll their balls.

strike
When a player knocks down all of the pins on their first ball.

Index

To Learn More

Learning more is as easy as 1, 2, 3.

1) Go to www.factsurfer.com

2) Enter "bowling" into the search box.

3) Click the "Surf" button to see a list of websites.